THIS BOOK BELONGS TO:

____

____

____

COLOR TEST

PEACE

PEACE
and
LOVE

<a href="https://www.vecteezy.com/free-vector/psychedelic">Psychedelic Vectors by Vecteezy</a>

<a href="https://www.vecteezy.com/free-vector/abstract">Abstract Vectors by Vecteezy</a>

<a href="https://www.vecteezy.com/free-vector/psychedelic-pattern">Psychedelic Pattern Vectors by Vecteezy</a>

<a href='https://www.freepik.com/free-photos-vectors/computer'>Computer vector created by macrovector - www.freepik.com</a>

<a href="https://www.freepik.com/free-photos-vectors/background">Background vector created by visnezh - www.freepik.com</a>

<a href="https://www.vecteezy.com/free-vector/catalog">Catalog Vectors by Vecteezy</a>

<a href="https://www.freepik.com/free-photos-vectors/floral">Floral vector created by freepik - www.freepik.com</a>

<a href="https://www.freepik.com/free-photos-vectors/flower">Flower vector created by visnezh - www.freepik.com</a>

<a href="https://www.vecteezy.com/free-vector/floral-pattern">Floral Pattern Vectors by Vecteezy</a>

<a href="https://www.vecteezy.com/free-vector/rasta">Rasta Vectors by Vecteezy</a>

<a href="https://www.vecteezy.com/free-vector/car-sticker">Car Sticker Vectors by Vecteezy</a>

<a href="https://www.vecteezy.com/free-vector/undefined">Undefined Vectors by Vecteezy</a>

<a href="https://www.vecteezy.com/free-vector/colorful">Colorful Vectors by Vecteezy</a>

<a href="https://www.vecteezy.com/free-vector/psychedelic">Psychedelic Vectors by Vecteezy</a>

<a href="https://www.vecteezy.com/free-vector/psychedelic">Psychedelic Vectors by Vecteezy</a>

<a href="https://www.vecteezy.com/free-vector/mythology">Mythology Vectors by Vecteezy</a>

<a href="https://www.vecteezy.com/free-vector/psychedelic">Psychedelic Vectors by Vecteezy</a>

<a href="https://www.vecteezy.com/free-vector/peace">Peace Vectors by Vecteezy</a>

<a href="https://www.vecteezy.com/free-vector/head">Head Vectors by Vecteezy</a>

<a href="https://www.vecteezy.com/free-vector/coloring">Coloring Vectors by Vecteezy</a>

<a href="https://www.vecteezy.com/free-vector/red">Red Vectors by Vecteezy</a>

<a href='https://www.freepik.com/free-photos-vectors/flower'>Flower vector created by raftel - www.freepik.com</a>